Elizabeth Jean

SIN IN THE CAMP
WHAT'S WRONG WITH THE CHURCH

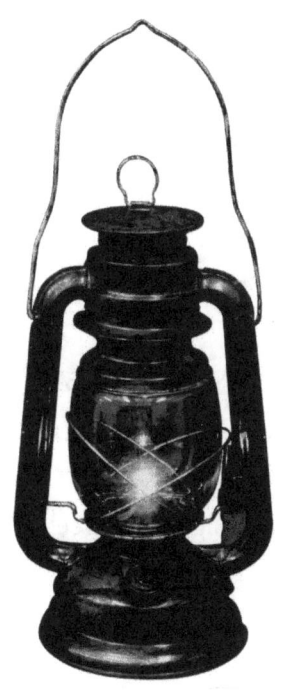

Sin in the Camp
What's Wrong with the Church
Copyright © 2022 Elizabeth Jean

All rights reserved. No part of this publication may be reproduced, distributed or transmitted in any form or by any means, without prior written permission.

Published by
Dreamer Reign Media, LLC
P.O. Box 291354
Port Orange, FL 32129

www.dreamerreign.com

For Worldwide Distribution
Printed in the U.S.A.

ISBN: 9781952253201
Library of Congress Control Number:

Cover Design: C Marcel Wiggins

TABLE OF CONTENTS

Introduction 4

Chapter One: Giving 7

Chapter Two: Salvation 19

Chapter Three: Word of Faith 29

Chapter Four: Prayer 43

Chapter Five: Forgiveness 55

Chapter Six: False Teachers 67

Chapter Seven: Unity: Part One 81

Chapter Eight: Unity: Part Two 91

Chapter Nine: Prophecy 105

Epilogue 110

INTRODUCTION

The Church has failed the body of Christ. It seems as though the Church leaders do not care whether or not people get their needs met. They seem to care about members and pet projects. In this book, I hope to show how the Church has failed, and what can be done about it.

I will address how the Church does not truly care for the poor. There is a lot of backbiting and gossip in the Church which needs to stop. There are abuses in the Word of Faith movement that need to be addressed. Young believers need to be allowed to grow and mature at their own pace. There is a movement out there that is very dangerous. We will address it and show why it is wrong. Leaders need to be honest before God and their congregations, as they preach the truth. The body is in disunity and needs to come together before the Lord. The Lord has a Word to say to the Church.

As we look at these issues, we hope to find solutions that are workable. It is important to realize presenting problems without presenting answers is nothing more than gripe sessions; that is useless. God does not want us to complain, He wants us to pray and seek answers.

"Be careful for nothing; but in everything by prayer and supplication with thanksgiving let your request be made known unto God." Philippians 4:6

In other words, stop griping and talk to God. He always has the answer.

All Scripture is taken from the King James Bible. If the reader wishes to use another version to get a better understanding of what is said, go ahead. My goal is to communicate the need to change, not be a stick in the mud. I want the reader to be clear about what I am saying and have an solution to each problem.

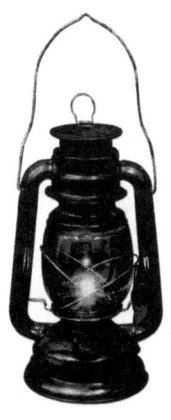

CHAPTER ONE
Giving

The Church seems to be more concerned about helping the less fortunate overseas than the less fortunate in this country; they turn a blind eye to the needs here. They have many excuses, but no real reasons to avoid helping.

In this chapter, I hope to look at some of these excuses scripturally, while offering some answers to the problem.

While there are desperate needs overseas, we must not turn a blind eye to the needs here at home. Too often, we treat the less fortunate at home as though they were a nuisance who should know better. We feel those overseas really need our help because of various reasons, such as: natural disasters, war, or other problems. While we do help the less fortunate in the U.S. in times of disasters, we tend to forget them on a daily basis.

"And all that believed were together and had all things in common; and sold their possessions and goods, and parted them to all men as every man had need." Acts 2:44, 45

"Neither was there any among them that lacked: for as many as were possessors of lands or houses sold them, and them, and brought the prices of the things that were sold, and laid them down at the apostles' feet: and distribution was made unto every man according as had need." Acts 4:34,35

While these verses refer to believers in the Church, I will remind my readers, the less fortunate are in the Church as well as in the world. It should not matter where the need is, just meet it. It is possible we may win the world to the Lord through our generosity.

CHAPTER ONE: GIVING

"What doth it profit, my brethren, though a man say he hath faith, and have not works? Can faith save him? If a brother or sister be naked and destitute of daily food, one of you say unto them, Depart in peace, be ye warmed and filled, not withstanding ye give them not those things which are needful to the body, what doth it profit?" James 2:14-16

"Hereby perceive we the love of God, because he laid down his life for us: and we ought to lay down our lives for the brethren. But whoso hath this world's good, and seeth his brother have a need and shutteth up his bowels of compassion, from him, how dwelleth the love of God in him? My little children, let us not love in word, neither in tongue; but in deed and in truth." 1 John 3:16-18

It is very clear from these verses, if we do not care for the less fortunate, our faith is worthless. We are not walking in love when we refuse to acknowledge their needs. Too often, we claim to have great faith and love, but we turn our back on their needs. We feel if they would just try harder, budget better, etc, the less fortunate would not need the help. While those thoughts may be right to a certain extent, they do not meet the immediate need.

What are some of the reasons the Church won't help? Some say there are too many to reach or bother. If we can reach one, we can make a difference in that person's life. As was said before, we do not know if we will reach the person for the Lord.

Some use scripture to create more problems for those who are in need.

"For even we were with you, this we commanded you, that if any would not work, neither should he eat." 2 Timothy 3:10

"But if any provide not for his own, and especially those of his own house, he hath denied the faith, and is worse than an infidel." 1 Timothy 5:8

These scriptures are used as clubs to condemn the less fortunate rather than encourage them. We recognize the importance to work or just start a new job. Yet, while they are either looking, or are just starting the job, they need assistance. Besides, there are those who cannot work because of mental and physical disabilities. They need special help while they are seeking help from the government. We need to be careful not to lump everyone into the same category.

Others complain the less fortunate will dirty up their churches. So what! The Bible does not say anything about how the Church should be protected from dirt. We need to remember the Church is not the building but individuals. We cannot clean up the people unless we help them. The building is merely the place where people meet and care for one another. The building can be cleaned up; the people need help, regardless.

Sadly, we as believers, think it is okay to take care of the people who are overseas because "they have the greatest need." We ignore the obvious needs in our country because there are so many resources here to meet the needs in every area, or so we believe. However, this is not true. Most, if not all less fortunate, are unskilled and need training so they can have steady jobs. They need help in getting that training and help to support their families.

I want to offer a program that will help the people get back on their feet. I want them to have some pride in themselves and confidence so they can realize they can succeed. There are four steps to the program.

1. The clients will initially receive help.

2. The clients will get counseling and help to get jobs which include necessary training.

3. After a specific period of time, the clients will receive counseling before they receive any further help.

4. Once the clients receive a job, they will receive additional assistance until they get their first paycheck.

This program will help those who are able to work, and still need help. The senior citizens, those with temporary medical needs, and the disabled need help on a constant basis far beyond what is offered to the able-bodied people. As a result, exceptions must be made for them. Some people have no one to help them care for themselves. If there are able-bodied people living in the homes, the following program will apply to them.

Senior citizens and the disabled, who are living alone, will have an unlimited amount of help to get them through the month. Those who

CHAPTER ONE: GIVING

have temporary medical needs, who live alone, will have the same privilege as the senior citizens and disabled to unlimited help, as long as a doctor deems it necessary.

1. The clients initially receive help.

First time clients may come in and get help from the agency over the next three months. After that, they will need additional help. Want ads and flyers for jobs will be strewed about the tables for the clients to look at and follow up to locate gainful employment. If the clients find and enroll in training to learn a job skill, they may receive additional help while they are in training.

2. The clients will receive counseling and help to obtain jobs with the necessary training.

While the clients get help for their basic needs, they will be given counseling as to how to obtain a job. They will be taught basic life skills like grooming, proper clothing care, and how to secure transportation for work. They will show efforts by looking for work and having prospective employers sign forms indicating the client has inquired about a job at their company. If training is needed, the clients will speak to prospective schools about enrollment and financial aid. Once they are employed or in training, they will move to step 4.

3. After a specific period of time, the clients will receive counseling before they receive further help.

If the clients have not been able to find employment, and are truly diligently looking for work, they will receive counseling as to how to manage their finances so they will not necessarily need to go to the agency many times. If they are not truly diligently looking, counseling will be given as to why and how the agency can help the client.

4. Once the client locates a job, they will receive further help until they get their first paycheck.

The client who locates a job will feel very successful. They will still need assistance for a short period of time. Once they receive a paycheck, they will no longer receive assistance.

This program is for those who are looking for work. We recognize there are those who do work, but do not make enough money to meet all their needs and their families' needs. In that case, we will help the clients take care of their needs. We also

CHAPTER ONE: GIVING

want to help them find more gainful employment, that will pay better so they can take care of their families properly.

One thing I want to make clear. We do not offer these services for free. Each client will be expected to do something to earn the help they receive. In this way, they will feel more self-confident and have more self-respect in themselves. One of the things we want to do is make sure the counselors have compassion and concern for each client and their families. The counselors need to realize they could be in the same position as the ones they serve, if they have not already been in that position.

Clients have more than food or clothing needs. They may be moving into a new home and need furniture and appliances. They may need help in getting nonfood supplies such as cleaning supplies, toilet paper, toiletries, dog food, etc. When the clients ask for help, the counselors need to make sure they find out all the needs of the clients. In this way, all the needs of the clients will be met.

It is understood that all churches or ministers can't do everything. However, the Word of God instructs us to do something! If we refuse to do anything, we are in disobedience to the Lord; all disobedience is sin.

CHAPTER ONE: GIVING

Your **REFLECTIONS**

_____

_____

_____

_____

_____

_____

_____

_____

_____

_____

_____

_____

_____

_____

SIN IN THE CAMP

CHAPTER TWO
Salvation

There is a movement out there founded by a pastor because he did not want to admit his family member was going to Hell. He teaches that everyone is going to heaven regardless of whether they accept Jesus or not. He disregards the scriptures that teach otherwise. He also teaches there is no hell to shun because everyone goes straight to heaven.

"I say unto you my friends, be not afraid of them that kill the body and after that have no more they can do. I will forewarn you whom you shall fear: Fear him, which after he has killed has power to cast into hell; I say unto you, Fear him."

Luke 12:4, 5

"There was a certain rich man which was clothed in purple and fine linen, and fared sumptuously every day. There was a certain beggar named Lazarus, which was laid at his gate, full of sores. Desiring to be fed with the crumbs which fell from the rich man's table: moreover the dogs came and licked his sores. It came to pass, that the beggar died, and was carried by the angels into Abraham's bosom: the rich man also died, and was buried. In hell, he lifted up his eyes, being in torments, seeing Abraham afar off and Lazarus in his bosom. He cried and said, Father Abraham, have mercy on me and send Lazarus that he may dip the finger in water, and cool my tongue for I am tormented in this flame. Abraham said, Son, remember that thou in thy lifetime received thy good things, and likewise Lazarus evil things but now he is comforted, and thou are tormented.

CHAPTER TWO: SALVATION

Beside all this, between us and you there is a great gulf fixed: so that they which would pass from hence to you cannot; neither can they pass to us that would come from thence. Then he said, I pray thee therefore, father that though would send him to my father's house. For I have five brethren; that he may testify unto them, lest they also come into this place of torment. Abraham said to him, they have Moses and the prophets, let them hear them. He said, nay, father Abraham: but if one went to them from the dead, they will repent. He said to him, if they hear not Moses and the prophets neither will be persuaded though one rose from the dead. Luke 16:19-31

In the first verse, Jesus makes it clear the only one we need to fear is the one who has the authority to send someone to hell. He is talking about His Father. The Father makes the final decision based on our final choice as to whether we will accept Jesus as Lord or not.

In the second verse, Jesus is telling a story of someone who is in Hell and what he desires to happen. This story is not a parable, but an actual incident. Every other parable never gave an exact name of any of the individuals discussed. In this story, a specific individual is named. I firmly believe this is a clear description of Hell. To say this is not real is to deny

SIN IN THE CAMP

the reality of the scriptures. In various scriptures, Jesus describes the horror of Hell. He says it is a place of wailing and gnashing of teeth. Anyone who tries to deny this is denying the very scriptures.

"For God so loved the world that he gave his only begotten Son that whosoever believes in him should not perish, but have everlasting life. For God sent not his Son into the world to condemn the world; but that the world through him might be saved. He that believeth on him is not condemned: but he that believeth not is condemned already, because he has not believed in the name of the only begotten Son of God. John 3:16-18

"For all have sinned, and come short of the glory of God." Romans 3:23

"For the wages of sin is death; but the gift of God is eternal life through Jesus Christ our Lord."

Romans 6:23

"If you shall confess with your mouth the Lord Jesus, and shall believe in your heart that God has raised him from the dead, you shall be saved. For with the heart man believes unto righteousness; and with the mouth confession is made unto salvation."

CHAPTER TWO: SALVATION

Romans 10:9, 10

In a nutshell, that is the message of salvation. It is acknowledging that God loved us and gave us His Son for us. It is admitting we are sinners. We have to confess Jesus as Lord to be saved. In other words, we have to do something to be saved.

We cannot just simply die and expect to go to Heaven without doing anything about it. Jesus made it very clear throughout the Gospels that we have to consciously decide what to do with Him.

This teaching that we do not have to do anything to go to Heaven is very dangerous. It sends millions of people to Hell because they believe all they have to do is live, die, and go to Heaven. It simply does not work that way.

Another wrong and dangerous teaching that is being taught... "all we have to do is perform enough good works to make it to heaven." The scripture teaches otherwise.

"For by grace are you saved through faith; and that not of yourselves: it is the gift of God. Not of works, lest any man should boast." Ephesians 2:8, 9

SIN IN THE CAMP

As this verse states, it is the grace of God that saves us, not anything we may or may not do. No matter how many good works we may do, the one bad thing wipes out all the good we may do.

"When I say unto the wicked, you shall surely die; and give him no warning, nor speak to warn the wicked from his wicked way, to save his life; the same wicked man shall die in his iniquity; but his blood will I require at your hands. Yet if you warn the wicked and he turn not from his wickedness, nor from his wicked way, he shall die in his iniquity; but you delivered your soul. Again, when a righteous man does turn from his righteousness, and commit iniquity, and I lay a stumbling block before him, he shall die: because you have not given him warning, he shall die in his sin, and his righteousness which he has done shall not be remembered; but his blood will I require at your hand. Nevertheless if you warn the righteous man, that he sin not, and he doth not sin, he shall surely live, because he was warned; also you have delivered your soul."

Ezekiel 3:18-21

"The soul that sins, it shall die. The son shall not bear the iniquity of the father, neither shall the father bear the iniquity of the son: the righteousness of the righteous

CHAPTER TWO: SALVATION

shall be upon him, and the wickedness of the wicked shall be upon him. But if the wicked will turn from his sins that he committed, and keep all my statutes, and do that which is lawful and right, he shall surely live, he shall not die. All his transgressions that he hath committed, they shall not be mentioned to him: in his righteousness that he has done he shall live. Have I any pleasure at all that the wicked should die? Says the Lord God: and not that he should return from his ways and live? But when the righteous turns away from his righteousness, and commits iniquity, and does according to all the abominations that the wicked man does shall he live? All his righteousness that has done shall not be mentioned: in his trespass that he has trespassed, and in his sin that he has sinned, in them shall he die." Ezekiel 18:20-24

In the first passage, we are to warn the sinners of their sins. If we do not, we are held accountable for what happens to them. If we see the righteous doing wrong, we must warn them or again we are held accountable. It is our job to warn so people can turn from their wrongdoing.

In the second passage, we see the sins of the father are imputed to the son or vice versa. Each is responsible as to what they are going to do. We are each held accountable for our behavior: we cannot blame it on others.

In both passages, we see one important fact. What was done good or evil in the past, is forgotten, and the good or evil is now done. When we try to say our good works will outweigh the bad, we are going against scripture. It is obvious when we do wrong, all our good works are forgotten. It is sad, but the world has gotten the Church to believe good work is all that is necessary. However, the Scriptures teach otherwise.

CHAPTER TWO: SALVATION

Your **REFLECTIONS**

SIN IN THE CAMP

CHAPTER **THREE**
Word of Faith

While the Word of Faith movement is a good one, it has errors that need to be corrected. It tends to push confession to the point of denying the real issue. Too often, the person is taught to ignore if not deny the actual problem or symptoms. The leaders of the movement teach that to acknowledge the issues is to deny the Lord the ability to work. They insist it is doubt and unbelief when the person acknowledges the problem.

This flies in the face of the scripture. In every individual healing, the illness was acknowledged.

Blind Bartimaeus was identified as blind.

> *"And they came to Jericho: and he went of Jericho with his disciples and a great number of people, blind Bartimaeus, the son of Timaeus sat by the highway side begging."*
>
> *Mark 10:46 (Emphasis mine)*

The man sick of the palsy was identified as having palsy.

> *"And behold, they brought to him a man sick of the palsy lying on a bed…" Matthew 9:2 (Emphasis mine)*

The leper was identified as a leper.

> *"And behold, there came a leper and worshipped him, saying Lord, if thou will, you can make me clean." Matthew 8:2*

David spoke of being depressed and anxious.

> *"Return O Lord, deliver my soul: oh save me for your mercies' sake. For in death there is no*

CHAPTER THREE: WORD OF FAITH

remembrance of you, in the grave who shall give you thanks. I am weary with my groaning; all the night make I my bed to swim, I water my couch with my tears. Mine eye is consumed because of grief; it waxes old because of all my enemies. I realize David does not use the word depressed or anxious but his comments in the Psalms indicate the emotion he is feeling." Psalms 6:4-7

The point is each person was identified as having a sickness or demon possession. When we say we do not have a sickness like high blood pressure, or depression, or any other problem we are ignoring the very Word of God and calling it a liar.

Now it is true, we need to be sure that we do not own the problem, but we need to be sure we allow the Lord to come and clear out the problem. We are not owning the problem. The sad thing is too many of us own the problem, yet expecting the Lord to heal us.

Now I have no problem with confession, but it can become a rote practice with no real feeling in it. It is as though it becomes a head practice and not a heart practice. We need to stop allowing the enemy to make fun of us because we have gotten away from a heartfelt practice of confession.

Another issue with confession is people thinking they can just think the scriptural confessions, without the actual speaking of it. We have to speak the Word of God out loud so we can hear it, the enemy can hear it, and the Lord hears it. For example: Matthew 10:32 says:

"Whoever therefore shall confess me before men, him will I confess also before my Father which is in heaven."

"That if you shall confess with your heart that God has raised him from the dead, you shall be saved. For with the heart man believeth to righteousness; and with the mouth confession is made unto salvation." Romans 10:9,10

While these verses refer to salvation, the people use them to confess the Word for the problem.

Another issue in the Word of Faith Movement is the fact most teachers do not link forgiveness with faith. They quote Mark 11:22-24 and ignore <u>verses 25 and 26.</u>

The entire passage reads as follows.

CHAPTER THREE: WORD OF FAITH

"And Jesus answering said unto them, have faith in God. For truly I say to you, that whoever shall say unto this mountain, you be removed and you be cast into the sea; and shall not doubt in his heart, but shall believe that those things which he says shall come to pass, he shall have whatever he says. Therefore I say to you, what things you desire, when you pray, believe that you receive them, and you shall have them. And when you stand praying, forgive, if you have anything against any: that your Father also which is in heaven may forgive you your trespasses. But if you do not forgive, neither will your Father which is in heaven forgive your trespasses." (Emphasis is mine.)

Note the word(Added quotation marks around "And") "And." It is a conjunction uniting the first three verses with the second two. In other words, Jesus did not end the thought at verse 24. He continued the thought of forgiveness in the next two verses. Too many leaders ignore this because they do not want to admit that is a very important fact. While they push faith to the point of ridiculousness, they forget the whole truth.

We cannot take scripture out of context and expect to be blessed. While it is important to speak the truth, we need to keep the scripture in context knowing that we are obeying the Word totally. In all the problems with the Word of Faith movement, it seems as though many Christians and religious leaders try to twist the Scripture to fit their pet doctrines and ignore what the Lord actually says.

While it is true, we have been forgiven through what Jesus did on the cross, we need to realize there are consequences to our refusal to forgive those who hurt us. While it is very important to speak to the mountain, we cannot ignore the rest of the information the Lord has given us. Paul even teaches forgiveness of one another.

The sad thing is, we want to hold onto our sacred cows and walk in unforgiveness thinking the blood covers it. We seem to believe that as long as we confess the blood over our lives, we do not have to forgive one another. We can hold grudges and hurt one another all under the guise of believing the blood of Jesus covers all the problems.

While this is a prayer issue as well, I believe the leaders of the Word of Faith movement forget they cannot take scriptures and either ignore them

CHAPTER THREE: WORD OF FAITH

or twist them to fit their pet teachings. Too often, we find different leaders take the scripture and try to teach things that are not there. As they do, they are guilty of trying to remove Scriptures that do not fit their pet doctrines.

On the opposite side of the Word of Faith are those who do not believe the Lord wants to bless the body of Christ. They do not feel the Church needs money. They believe the Church can survive with the help of the Lord.

They do not realize unbelievers are not impressed with how much faith the believers have. They need money to pay the bills. No landlord, bank, utility company, or other creditor will give them what they need for free. The creditors need finances to take care of the bills.

The way these people believe, it seems as though they expect money to fall from heaven. They seem to think God is up in heaven printing all the money that comes down from heaven to pay the bills. The problem with that thinking is that makes the Lord a major criminal and thus a sinner. They do not acknowledge the fact that the Lord uses people to meet the needs. Even if they do, they see the Lord as very stingy. They see him as demanding, but not blessing the givers.

Too often they ignore the stories of Abraham, David, Solomon, and others who were greatly blessed. If they acknowledge these stories, they put them in the past as irrelevant today. When it is pointed out there are people who are blessed today in their finances, they make up the excuse that the people must be doing something wrong to get such wealth. They just do not want to admit the Lord wants to bless His children.

"Will a man rob God? Yet you have robbed me. But you say, wherein have we robbed you? In tithes and offerings. You are cursed with a curse: for you have robbed me, even this whole nation. You bring all the tithes into the storehouse, that there may be meat in my house, and prove me herewith, says the Lord of hosts, if I will not open you the windows of heaven and pour you out a blessing, that there shall not room to receive it. And I will rebuke the devourer for your sakes, and he shall not destroy the fruits of your ground; neither shall your vine cast her fruit before the time in the field, says the Lord of hosts." Malachi 3:8-11 (Emphasis mine)

"Honor the Lord with your substance, and with the

CHAPTER THREE: WORD OF FAITH

firstfruits of all your increase: so shall your barns be filled with plenty and thy presses shall burst out with new wine." Proverbs 3:9,10 (Emphasis mine)

"He which sows sparingly shall also reap sparingly; and he which sows bountifully shall also reap also bountifully. Every man according as he purposes in his heart, so let him give; grudgingly, or of necessity: for God loves a cheerful giver. And God is able to make all grace abound toward you; that you, always having all sufficiency in all things, may abound to every good work: (As it is written, he has dispersed abroad; he has given to the poor; his righteousness remains forever. Now he that ministers seed to the sower both minister bread for your food, and multiply your seed sown, and increase the fruits of your righteousness;)"2 Corinthians 9: 6-10 (Emphasis mine)

"For even in Thessalonica you sent once and again to my necessity. Not because I desire a gift: but I desire fruit may abound to your account. But I have all, and abound: I am full having received of Epaphroditus the things which were sent from you, an odor of a sweet smell, a sacrifice acceptable, well pleasing to God. But my God shall supply all your need according to his riches in glory by Christ Jesus." Philippians 4:16-19 (Emphasis mine)

SIN IN THE CAMP

In these verses, we see the promise of the Lord to bless us as we give him our finances. To say otherwise is to do violence to the scripture. Anyone who teaches otherwise is either ignorant of the Word of God or enjoys keeping people in bondage. I listed two scriptures from the Old Testament and two scriptures from the New Testament to prove the entire Bible teaches the necessity to expect prosperity from the Lord. I am not saying the giver will be made super rich from giving, but I am saying he or she will have their needs met to an overflowing manner so they can bless others in their times of need.

We need to have a balance of the Word of Faith or prosperity doctrine. We need to be careful to be totally honest with the Father about our needs. We are not to deny the symptoms, but rather acknowledge the problem. As we do, we will see the Lord meet our needs. On the other hand, we are not to deny the blessings from the Lord who desires to meet us and bless us. We need to realize the Church needs to receive finance from the body to run the work the Lord wants to run.

I am not saying to seek the Lord for the

blessings, that puts Him in the place of an indulgent daddy who will give us everything we want, even to our hurt. We need to realize the Lord knows what is best for us. We also need to understand the enemy will bring things in that will cause us great harm. We have to trust the Lord to meet us right where we are and bless us with what He knows we need.

SIN IN THE CAMP

CHAPTER THREE: WORD OF FAITH

Your **REFLECTIONS**

_____
_____
_____
_____
_____
_____
_____
_____
_____
_____
_____
_____
_____
_____

SIN IN THE CAMP

CHAPTER **FOUR**
Prayer

Prayer is very important to the body of Christ. It is a two-way communication with the Father. It is a time when we talk to the Father about our lives and our situations. It is also a time when we listen to the small still voice of the Lord to give us direction for our lives.

Too much prayer is begging and pleading as if we think the Lord cannot hear us unless we grovel at His feet. Too many of us feel the Lord is so busy or is so inept, He cannot hear us or does not care. We feel as though if we do not go into great detail, He is unable to understand the severity of the situation. We feel we have to explain over and over to the Father because He is either deaf or totally inept to figure out what we actually need.

The Father is present everywhere, all-powerful, and all-knowing. He is greater than we are. Because He is quite capable of understanding what we need and when we need it, He is capable of meeting us where we are.

"For my thoughts are not your thoughts, neither are your ways my ways, says the Lord. For as the heavens are higher than the earth, so are my ways higher than your ways, and my thoughts than your thoughts. For as the rain comes down, and the snow from heaven, and returns not there, but waters the earth, and makes it bring forth and bud, that it may give seed to the sower, and bread to the eater. So shall my word be that goes forth out of mouth; it shall not prosper in the thing whereto I sent it." Isaiah 55:8-11 (Emphasis mine)

What we need to realize is that the Lord sees things in a different way than we do. He knows the end from the beginning. He knows what we need to bless us and meet our needs. When we come to Him as groveling little children, we insult Him.

CHAPTER FOUR: PRAYER

"Ask, and and it shall be given you; seek, and you shall find; knock, and it shall be opened to you. For everyone that asks receives, and he that seeks, finds; and to him that knocks it shall be opened. Or what man is there of you, whom if his son ask bread, will he give him a stone? Or if he ask a fish, will he give him a serpent? If you then, being evil, know how to give good gifts to your children, how much more shall your father which is in heaven give good things to them that ask him?" Matthew 7:7-11 (Emphasis mine)

In other words, the Father wants to give us what we need daily. The problem is us. We do not think He will do it. If a parent did what Jesus suggests, he would be guilty of child abuse. Yet, we are accusing the Lord of the same thing.

We do not have to grovel at His feet, we must come to Him as loving children and ask.

While ask means to ask and keep on asking, we need to realize the Lord already knows what we need. The asking is to understand what we are asking for. Just like the child who asks for bread, he does not keep pleading for the bread. He asks fully expecting to receive what the Lord wants to give him. The problem is, we really do not believe the

Father wants to meet our needs.

We look at the Lord's Prayer and recognize the Lord as Father and spend time loving on Him. We must stop groveling. When we ask, it is a short thought to speak to a specific need and return to praising Him and loving on Him.

"After this manner therefore you pray: Our Father which art in heaven, hallowed be your name. Your kingdom come, your will be done in earth, as it is in heaven. Give us this day our daily bread. And forgive us our debts, as we forgive our debtors. And lead us not into temptation, but deliver us from evil: For yours is the kingdom, and the power, and the glory forever. Amen."

Matthew 6:9-13 (Emphasis mine)

We need to realize Jesus never intended to make the prayer a rote prayer to be recited at the will of the Church. It is a model for us to follow. It is an example for us to use. We need to realize the Lord Jesus wants us to understand we do not need to use vain repetitions as the hypocrites use.

While I understand this was given before the crucifixion, I believe we can apply it to us today. I believe we need to understand the point

CHAPTER FOUR: PRAYER

Jesus is making. He wants us to come to Him in humility, recognizing the Father is Holy and to be worshipped. As we love on the Father, we will see our needs met. As we do this, we will see the Lord meet us where we are.

"Be careful for nothing; but in everything by prayer and supplication with thanksgiving let your requests be made known to God. And the peace of God, which passes all understanding, shall keep your hearts and minds through Christ Jesus."

Philippians 4:6,7 (Emphasis mine)

We are to remember to take all our needs to the Lord, but we are to thank Him for what He does. Too often, we make demands of Him, expecting Him to meet our needs. We would not treat our parents or family that way. We would ask and say please and thank you (to the best of our ability).

There are four ways we come to the Father. We treat the Father as a computer where we push buttons and expect a read out of what we demanded. We treat Him as a bellhop that jumps to our every whim. We do not expect Him to meet our needs, unless we grovel, beg, and plead. We confidently go to Him knowing He will meet us where we are.

The Father is not a computer or a bellhop. He is the almighty God; Who desires to meet us halfway. As mentioned above, His ways are not like ours nor are His thoughts like our thoughts. We need to realize the Father desires to meet us right where we are and take care of us. We need to respect Him as Father and treat Him as a loving Daddy who desires to take care of us.

When we insist on groveling, begging, and pleading, we are calling the loving Father a monster and a child abuser. We are listening to the lies of the enemy who wants to convince us that God does not really love us or have our best interests at heart. We need to tell the enemy to take a flight and shut up.

The best response we can have to the Father is to come before Him confidently. We have nothing to worry about. We know He desires to meet us where we are at. We have stopped the lies of the enemy from affecting us. We recognize the Father knows before we ask what we have need of.

CHAPTER FOUR: PRAYER

"And he spoke a parable to them to this end, that men ought always to pray, and not to faint; saying, there was in a city a judge, which feared not God, neither regarded man: And there was widow in that city; and she came to him, saying, avenge me of my adversary. And he would not for a while: but afterward he said within himself, though I fear not God, nor regard man; yet because this widow troubles me, I will avenge her, lest by her continual coming she weary me. And the Lord said, Hear what the unjust judge says. And shall not God avenge his own elect, which cry day and night unto him, though he bear long with him? I tell you that he will avenge them speedily. Nevertheless when the Son of Man comes, shall he find faith on the earth."
Luke 18:1-8

Just as Jesus said to ask and keep on asking, He is teaching here to consistently pray so as to be heard. This does not mean to grovel at his feet, but with love mention the need to the Father. We are to not stop praying regardless of the specific situation.

"Rejoice evermore. Pray without ceasing. In everything give thanks: for this is the will of God in Christ Jesus concerning you."

Thessalonians 5:16-18 (Emphasis mine)

SIN IN THE CAMP

We are to cover all prayer with joy and thanksgiving. Understand this does not mean we are to stay on our knees or our prayer closets constantly. That would be impractical. We have to live our daily lives. We have to eat, sleep, etc. We have to talk with people on a daily basis. We cannot use this as an excuse to avoid ministering to people with the Gospel.

I do not believe we need to shout to the Lord or to the enemy. They are not deaf. They are perfectly capable of hearing us. I feel the reason we do is to get attention from our audience. Apparently, the louder we get; the more the audience thinks we are extra spiritual. The same is true. The louder we get, the more we prove how insecure we really are. If we truly believed the Lord heard us, the quieter we would get. We do not holler at our family and friends because we know they can hear us. We need to have the same respect for the Lord. Now, it is true we may holler because we are angry, but after a point we need to calm down and realize the Lord will meet us where we are at.

I also know Jesus told us to ask for everything

CHAPTER FOUR: PRAYER

in His name. We are given authority in that Name. Jesus, in the last teaching He gave before the cross, taught that God, the Father gave authority in the name of Jesus. When we do not finish our prayers with, the Father stops listening. When we say, we are also refusing to honor the Name as it says. I realize we do not want to get into rote repetition, but when we do not we are disobeying the Father in our prayers. This, I believe, refers to public prayer. Private prayer involves a continual conversation in our hearts with the Father on a daily basis.

"If you shall ask anything in my name, I will do it." John 14:14

"And in that day ye shall ask me nothing. Truly, truly, I say to you, whatever you shall ask the Father in my name, he will give it to you. Hitherto, you have asked nothing in my name: ask, and you shall receive, that your joy may be full. These things have I spoken to you in proverbs: but the time comes when I shall show you plainly of the Father. At that day you shall ask in my name: and I say not to you, that I will pray the Father for you: For the Father himself loves you, because you have loved me, and have believed that I came out from God." John 16:23-27

SIN IN THE CAMP

CHAPTER FOUR: PRAYER

Your **REFLECTIONS**

_____

_____

_____

_____

_____

_____

_____

_____

_____

_____

_____

_____

_____

SIN IN THE CAMP

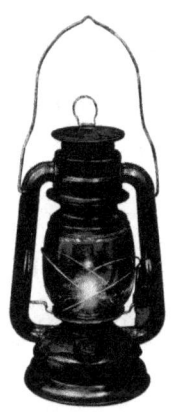

CHAPTER **FIVE**
FORGIVENESS

One issue that comes up is forgiveness. We think we can pray and talk to the Father with grudges in our hearts. We think that just because the Lord has forgiven us at Calvary, it absolves us from forgiving one another. Jesus makes it very clear as does Paul: forgiveness is absolutely necessary for our walk with the Lord.

"For if you forgive men their trespasses, your heavenly Father will also forgive you: but if you forgive not men their trespasses, neither will your Father forgive your trespasses." Matthew 6:14,15 (Emphasis mine)

"Then came Peter to him, and said, Lord, how oft shall my brother sin against me, and I forgive him? Till seven times? Jesus said unto him, I say not until seven times: but, until seventy times seven. Therefore is the king of heaven likened unto a certain king, which would take account of his servant. And when had begun to reckon, one was brought unto him, which owed him ten thousand talents. But forasmuch as he had not to pay, his lord commanded him to be sold, and his wife, and children, and all that he had, and payment to be made. The servant therefore fell down, and worshipped him, saying, Lord, have patience with me, and I will pay you all. Then the Lord of that servant was moved with compassion, and loosened him, and forgave him the debt. But the same servant went out, and found one of his fellow servants, which owed him an hundred pence: and he laid hands on him, and took him by the throat, saying, pay me that you owe. And his fellow servant fell down at his feet, and besought him, saying, have

CHAPTER FIVE: FORGIVENESS

patience with me, and I will pay you all. And he would not: but went and cast him into prison, till he should pay the debt. So when his fellow servants saw what was done, they were very sorry, and came and told their lord all that was done. Then his lord, after he had called him, said to him, O you wicked servant, I forgave all that debt, because you desired me: should not you also have had compassion on your fellow servant, even as I had pity on you? And his lord was wroth, and delivered him to the tormentors, till he should pay all that was due to him. So likewise shall my heavenly Father do also to you, if you from your hearts forgive not everyone his brother their trespasses." Matthew 18:21-35 (Emphasis mine)

"Take heed to yourselves: if your brother trespass against you, rebuke him; and if he repent, forgive him. And if he trespass against you seven times in a day turn again to you saying, I repent, you shall forgive him." Luke 17:3, 4 (Emphasis mine)

"Let all bitterness, and wrath, and anger, and clamor, and evil speaking, be put away from you, with all malice: and be kind to one another, tenderhearted, forgiving one another, even as God for Christ's sake has forgiven you." Ephesians 4:31, 32 (Emphasis mine)

SIN IN THE CAMP

In these scriptures, we see the importance of forgiving one another. It does not matter what has happened to us. People can be cruel, but we have an answer to that cruelty. We are commanded to walk in love and forgiveness. It is only as we realize that we are commanded to forgive will we truly find freedom.

I heard a minister, whom I truly respect; say. "we cannot forgive sins because we are not the Lord." While he is right in a way, he is wrong in another. We cannot forgive an individual's sin against the Lord or others. They are responsible for what they do. If they choose to walk in disobedience to the Lord, knowing what they are doing is wrong, that is between them and the Lord.

When the person causes us harm through abuse or mistreatment in any way, it causes us to stumble. We have to deal with the hurt and the consequences of that hurt. We must forgive them. It does not absolve them of the wrong they have done in our lives. It brings healing to us.

I heard a statement that I believe is very true. We cannot drink poison and expect it to kill the other person. The poison is going to kill us. In

CHAPTER FIVE: FORGIVENESS

other words, the person who has hurt us may not even know they hurt you. Even if they do, they do not really care. The poison is the bitterness we carry because of the nursed hurt. We never forget what was done. To keep remembering it and dragging it up as the reason we cannot move on, is to literally put the person in the place of God. It puts up a wall between us and the Lord.

This unforgiveness causes us great harm in so many ways. It affects us spiritually, emotionally, mentally, and physically. It hinders our prayers because we won't let go of the past. It hurts us emotionally because we carry around a grudge full of bitterness. It brings deep depression in our minds because all we can do is dwell on the hurt. Physically, it can cause high blood pressure and other sicknesses that cause us to suffer.

Now I am not saying it is that simple, or am I. Very often, when we free the person from the chains of unforgiveness we have bound about ourselves, we discover a new freedom and peace. Many of the problems we deal with will be relied in our lives. I am not saying physical and mental problems will be wiped out, but I am saying the effects will be lessened. When we are trying to run away from the problem, we are literally saying the Lord cannot help us.

In the story of the master and the two servants, we see the master forgiving the one servant a huge debt. When the servant comes upon another servant, he throws him in prison to force him to pay back the debt. As a result, he suffers the consequences of his refusal to extend the same mercy that was extended to him.

We need to understand this story is in response to the question asked by Peter. He asked how many times should he forgive someone who hurt him. He wanted to put limits on forgiveness. Just like us, he didn't want to be taken advantage of in this area. Jesus, in His response, made it clear there were no limits on forgiveness. We need to realize Jesus paid a great debt for our sins when He died on Calvary. He took all our sins and failures on the cross and died there, saying it is finished. Being finished means there is absolutely nothing we can add to or take away from that forgiveness. When we set limits, we are saying what Jesus did was not enough.

Going back to the parable, we need to realize that Jesus is comparing the difference between how much we are forgiven and how little we are forgiving others. We have been forgiven a great debt of sin in our lives. We have been made the righteousness of Christ and made new creations. When we choose to forgive others, we are saying what they did is nothing compared to what we are forgiven of.

We need to realize if we refuse to forgive, we suffer the consequences of unforgiveness. The tormentors mentioned in the parable are the enemies of our minds throwing accusations at us. When we are walking in unforgiveness, we are choosing to listen to those voices, instead of the still silent voice of the Lord. He wants to draw us out of our prison, but we would rather stay there thinking we are punishing the one who we refuse to forgive.

The sad thing is the person we refuse to forgive is not even affected by our behavior. He or she either does not care or even know what is wrong. They are often confused by what we are doing. Those who do not care will take advantage of us and hurt us more because to them it is funny.

When we choose to forgive, we are saying they have no more control over us. We are literally saying we are free because the pain has been removed from our hearts.

One thing we need to realize is that when we refuse to forgive, we are not just hurting ourselves; we are hurting those around us. Very often, they do not understand why we are so miserable, let alone know how to help us. They suffer silently in so many ways. The children we have get very rebellious and turn against the Lord because of our suffering. Our spouses often either give up and walk away or they stop interacting with us. We lose many friends because they see the dark cloud and do not know how to help us. The way out of this is to forgive those who have hurt us.

"Judge not, and ye shall not be judged: condemn not, and ye shall not be condemned: forgive, and ye shall be forgiven: give and it shall be given to you; good measure, pressed down, and shaken together, and running over, shall men give into your bosom. For with the same measure that you measure withal it shall be measured to you again." Luke 6:37, 38

This is the most misused scripture in the

CHAPTER FIVE: FORGIVENESS

Bible. Believers, (including me) use verse 38 to claim prosperity. We take the verse out of context. We say the Lord is going to bless us tremendously in so many ways, especially in finances through people. While it is true the Lord wants to prosper us, we need to realize the verse refers to the previous verse which says we are not to judge or condemn but rather forgive. That is what is measured by us to be measured against us in our lives. We need to realize that people will hurt us or forgive us in the same manner or greater manner than we have done to others. The more we give out these things, the more we will receive the same thing in our lives.

Let us turn the situation around and forgive one another so we may be forgiven. We need to realize it as we forgive; we open the door to the Lord to communicate to us so we can grow in him. When we refuse, we slam the door in the face of the Lord to love on us as much as He wants to. Let us keep the door open and walk out forgiveness.

SIN IN THE CAMP

CHAPTER FIVE: FORGIVENESS

Your **REFLECTIONS**

_____
_____
_____
_____
_____
_____
_____
_____
_____
_____
_____
_____
_____

SIN IN THE CAMP

CHAPTER SIX
False Teachers

The Bible says,

"Woe be unto the pastors that destroy and scatter the sheep of my pasture! Says the Lord. Therefore thus says the Lord God of Israel against the pastors that feed my people; you have scattered my flock and driven them away, and have not visited them: behold, I will visit upon you the evil of your doings, says the Lord. I will gather the remnant of my flock out of all the countries where I have driven them, and will bring again to their folds; and they shall fruitful and increase. I will set up shepherds over them which will feed them; and

SIN IN THE CAMP

they shall fear no more, nor be dismayed neither shall they be lacking, says the Lord. Behold the days come, says the Lord, that I will raise unto David a righteous branch, and a king shall reign and prosper, and shall execute judgment and justice in the earth." Jeremiah 23:1-6

"And the word of the Lord came unto me saying, Son of man, prophesy against the prophets of Israel that prophesy and you unto them that prophecy out of their own hearts, hear you the word of the Lord; thus says the Lord God, woe unto the foolish prophets that follow their own spirit, and have seen nothing! O Israel, your prophets are like the foxes in the deserts. You have not gone up into the gaps, neither made up the hedge for the house to stand in the battle in the day of the Lord. They have seen vanity and lying divination, saying, the Lord says, and the Lord has not sent them: and they have made others to hope that they would confirm the word. Have you not seen a vain vision, and have you not spoken a lying a divination, whereas you say, the Lord says it; albeit I have not spoken? Therefore thus says the Lord God; because you have spoken vanity, and seen lies, therefore, behold, I am against you, says the Lord God. My hand shall be upon the prophets that see vanity, and that divine lies: they shall not be in the assembly of my people;

CHAPTER SIX: FALSE TEACHERS

neither shall they be written in the writing of the house of Israel, neither shall they enter into the land of Israel; and you shall know that I am the Lord God." Ezekiel 13:1-9

"And the word of the Lord came to me saying, Son of Man prophesy against the shepherds of Israel, prophesy, and say to them, thus says the Lord God to the shepherds, Woe to be to the shepherds of Israel that do feed themselves! Should not the shepherds feed the flocks? You eat the fat, and you clothe you with the wool, you kill them that are fed; but you feed not the flock. The diseased you have not strengthened, neither have you bound up that which was broken, neither have you brought again that which was driven away, neither have you sought that which was lost; but with force and cruelty have you ruled them. They were scattered, because there is no shepherd, and they became meat to all the beasts of the field, when they were scattered. My sheep wandered through all the mountains, and every high hill: yes, my flock was scattered upon all the face and none did search or seek after them. Therefore you shepherds, hear the word of the Lord: As I live, says the Lord God, surely because my flock became a prey, and my flock became meat to every beast of the field, because there was no shepherd, neither did my

SIN IN THE CAMP

shepherds search for my flocks, but the shepherds fed themselves, and feed not my flock; therefore oh you shepherds, hear the word of the Lord; thus says the lord God, behold I am against the shepherd; and I will require my flock at their hand, and cause them to cease from feeding the flock, neither shall the shepherds feed themselves anymore; for I will deliver my flock from their mouth, that they may not be meat for them. The Lord God says; behold, I, even I, will both search my sheep, and seek them out. As a shepherd seeks out his flock in the day that he is among his sheep that are scattered; so I will seek my sheep, and will deliver them out of all places where they have been scattered in the cloudy and dark day." Ezekiel 34:1-12

"Woe unto you, scribes and Pharisee, hypocrites! You shut up the kingdom of heaven against men: for you neither go in yourselves, neither do you allow them that are entering to go in. Woe to you, scribes and Pharisees, hypocrites! You devour widows' houses, and for a pretense make long prayer: therefore you shall receive the greater damnation. Woe unto you, scribes and Pharisees, hypocrites! You compass sea and land to make one proselyte and when he is made, you make him twofold more the child of hell than yourselves." Matthew 23:13-15

"Preach the word; be instant in season, out

CHAPTER SIX: FALSE TEACHERS

of season; reprove, rebuke, exhort with all longsuffering and doctrine. For the time will come when they will not endure sound doctrine; but after their own lust shall heap to themselves having itching ears; they shall turn away their ears from the truth, and shall be turned to fables." 2 Timothy 4:2-4 (Emphasis mine)

From these above scriptures, we see the Lord is very angry. His leaders do not take care of his sheep the way He wants them to. He hates religious leaders who tear up the sheep and think it is funny. They hurt and wound the sheep in such a way as to literally starve them and kill them with their legalism. They preach to tickle ears so they can be sure of huge congregations and lots of money. They do not teach sound doctrine, but teach things that make their congregations feel good.

What are some examples of the false leaders? There are religious leaders who have been elected into their positions. They may not actually have the true call on their lives. They felt this would be an easy way to make money. They find it is really difficult; so they often quit because the demands are more than they can handle. These have not discovered that they were not truly called and walked away harming and hurting so many who looked to them for guidance.

Another problem is denominations that dictate what the religious leaders can preach and say. These are truly called people. They want to speak the total truth, but are afraid because the denominations pay their checks and provide them with places to live. They have families and want to provide for them. It is a sad thing when the denominations become the god to the leaders instead of the almighty God.

These ones need to have the courage to say no, and leave the denominations.

They became leaders because their parents were. The ones that inherited their positions often miss the struggle their parents went through so they fail. Now, I am not saying that all leaders who got their positions this way are not bad. They have been groomed by their parents to take over leadership by working from the bottom up and know what is really happening.

"Again the word of the Lord came unto me saying, Son of man, speak to the children of my people and

CHAPTER SIX: FALSE TEACHERS

say to them, when I bring the sword upon a land, if the people of the land take a man of their coasts, and set him for their watchman: if when he sees the sword come upon the land, he blow the trumpet, and warn the people; then whoever hears the sound of the trumpet, and takes not warning, if the sword come, and take him away, his blood shall be upon his own head. He heard the sound of the trumpet, and took not warning; his blood shall be upon him. He that takes warning shall deliver his soul. But if the watchman see the sword come and blow not the trumpet, and the people be not warned; if the sword come and take any person from among them, he is taken away in his iniquity; but his blood will I require at the watchman's hand. So you Oh Son of man, I have set you a watchman to the house of Israel; therefore you shall hear the word at my mouth, and warn them from me. When I say to the wicked, oh wicked man you shall surely die; if you do not speak to warn the wicked from his, that wicked man shall die in his iniquity; but his blood will I require at your hand. Nevertheless, if you warn the wicked of his way to turn from it; if he does not turn from his way, he shall die in his iniquity; but you have delivered your soul.

SIN IN THE CAMP

Therefore, oh Son of man, speak to the house of Israel; thus you speak, saying, if our transgressions and our sins be upon us, and we pine away in them, how should we then live? Say to them, As I live, says the Lord God, I have no pleasure in the death of the wicked; but that the wicked turn from his way and live: turn you, turn you from you evil ways; for why will you die, oh house of Israel? Therefore you son of man, say to the children of your people, the righteousness of the righteous shall not deliver him in the day of his transgression: as for the wickedness of the wicked, he shall not fall thereby in the day he turns from his wickedness; neither shall the righteous able to live for his righteousness in the day that he sins. When I shall say to the righteous that he shall surely live; if he trust to his own righteousness, and commit iniquity, all his righteousness shall not be remembered; but for his iniquity, he shall die for it. Again, when I unto the wicked, you shall not die; if he turn from his sin, and do that which is lawful and right; if the wicked restore the pledge, give again that he had robbed, walk in the statutes of life, without committing iniquity, he shall surely live. Yet the children of you people say, the way of the Lord is not equal: but as

CHAPTER SIX: FALSE TEACHERS

for them, their way is not equal. When the righteous turns from his righteousness and commits iniquity, he shall even die thereby. But if the wicked turn from his wickedness and do that which is lawful and right, he shall live thereby. Yet you say, the way of the Lord is not equal, oh house of Israel, I will judge everyone after his ways." Ezekiel 33:1-20

Religious leaders are called to be watchmen. They are to warn the flock when they are going astray so the flock can get back on track. If they do not do their jobs, many of the flock will be destroyed. When the warning is given and those who do not listen are led to destruction, the leaders are not responsible.

I have seen many interpret watchmen to be prophets, but I do not believe it is referring to prophets, but rather the local leaders. Prophets do not take care of local flocks because that is not their purpose. The local leaders, such as pastors, are the ones who minister to the local flocks. I believe prophets are called to the entire body of Christ, either in the region they live in or the entire nation where they live.

Later in the same chapter, Ezekiel described

the wicked who have turned to righteousness, and the righteous who have turned to wickedness. He said the people thought the Lord was unfair because they wanted the changes to be forgotten. The people rewarded or punished according to what they were before the change. The people wanted the Lord to judge the way they judged. The people ignore what Isaiah says in **Isaiah 55:8**: "For My thoughts are not your thoughts, Nor are your ways My ways," says the Lord. So, they make excuses for what is going on in the world. It is time to stop making excuses.

The false leaders try to ignore what the Word of God says and teach a perverted Gospel. They do not want their people to know the real truth of what Jesus did on Calvary. They do not want people to know there is a way out of their sins and difficulties. The leaders want to cover up the sin by programs and nice words that uplift the people. They refuse to call sin what it is — SIN! They want to make excuses for the sins and call them normal behaviors. The sad thing is these leaders are sending millions of people to Hell because of their false teachings. So many of the true flock are damaged and need healing. It is time to see a change in the body.

CHAPTER SIX: FALSE TEACHERS

The Lord promises to bring in new religious leaders who speak the Word of Truth. Though they might not be as popular at first, the true sheep of the Lord will flock to them. These leaders will bind up the brokenhearted and the hurt. They will restore them to a new higher walk that will cause them to truly know the Lord. The true leaders will call sin what it is — SIN! They will present the truth of Calvary and what Jesus did for the people.

Let us seek the Lord with all hearts for the truth to come out and teach people what we are to do. Let us pray for true called men and women to come forth and speak the whole truth, no matter who it hurts. We need to speak the truth in love, but we need to speak it.

SIN IN THE CAMP

CHAPTER SIX: FALSE TEACHERS

Your **REFLECTIONS**

SIN IN THE CAMP

CHAPTER **SEVEN**
Unity: Part One

My son in-law, Phillip, gave me this sermon to describe unity in the Church. I hope you see it as a response to what has been said before in the book.

Unity is so important to the function of any organization or group. Unity is especially important in the Church. Jesus knew that unity will be an issue for the followers.

"My prayer is not them alone. I pray for those who will believe in me through the message that all of them may be one. Father, just as you are in me and I in you. May they also be in us so that the world may believe that you sent me? I have given them the glory that you have sent me, that they may be one as we are one. I am in them and you in me. May they be brought to complete unity to let the world know sent me and have loved them even as you have loved me?" John 17:20-23

Today we are going to be studying Philippians 2:1-11. These verses concern the unity of the Church. The command Paul gives us is found in verse two.

"Fulfill my joy by being like minded having the same love, being of one accord, of one mind." Phillippians 2:2

This command which concerns the unity of the Church is often repeated in Scriptures. In Ephesians 4:13, it says make every effort to keep the unity of the Spirit through the bond of peace. In Romans 15:5-6 it says,

CHAPTER SEVEN: UNITY PART ONE

"may the God who gives endurance and encouragement give you a spirit of unity so with one heart and mouth you may glorify God."

Before we get to the command of verse two, we must first consider the basis of being untied. Verse one provides us with enough reason to remain united together. In verse one, Paul strings together four sentences with the word if.

1. If there is any consolation in Christ, if there is any comfort in Christ.

2. If any comfort of love. This refers to God's love for us.

3. If any fellowship in the Spirit.

4. If any have affection and mercy.

5. Paul spoke to us that we be united on the levels of these four things.

6. On the basis of the grace of Christ and the comfort we have in knowing him we are untied.

7. On the basis of the love of God that we have experienced we are united. The love of God which resulted in sending His Son Jesus Christ

to die on the cross for sinners.

8. On the basis of our being indwelt by the Holy Spirit, who empowers, gets us a guarantee of our salvation, we are to be united.

9. On the basis of our general and ongoing experience of the affection and mercy of God, we are to be united.

When we have all that God has done for us in mind and keep it in mind, then we will find ourselves staying united.

In verses three through five, Paul follows up the unity command in verse two with three commands.

1. Let nothing be done for selfish ambition or conceit, but in lowliness of mind, let each esteem others better than ourselves. When our motives are not pure and we carry an attitude of being better than others, the unity of the Church is at risk. We need to be careful about our motives. Sometimes a person seeks a ministry position because they want to be noticed. They want the authority that goes with the position. We need to have a servant's heart. Our motives should

CHAPTER SEVEN: UNITY PART ONE

always be to use our gifts and abilities for the benefit of others and not for selfish goals.

2. We should not only look at our interests but also the interests of others. Verse four is a neat verse. For one thing, looking after ourselves and pursuing our own interests is acknowledged as acceptable and good. However, the qualification is that we must also consider the interests of others. Verse four commands us to be concerned and more than just concerned, but to do something about the interests of others. Selfishness and self-concern is nothing new. We are not the first generation to be the "me generation." Paul says in Philippians 2:20, 21, I have no one else like Timothy who takes a genuine interest in your welfare. For everyone looks out for his own interests, not those of Jesus Christ. We have to care more than just for ourselves. Christian unity depends on this. The personal welfare and well-being of each other needs to be our concern. We need to get others focused and stop being stuck on ourselves, problems, and interests. We must become servants to each other. It means getting to know each other. To do that, we need to spend more

time than just Sunday mornings together. What does this lead to? It leads to acts of caring, expressions of love, intercessory prayer, regular Christian fellowship, and unity in the Church.

3. Be united by striving to have the same mind which was also in Christ Jesus, verses five through eleven. If we strive as we are commanded to adopt the mind of Jesus that is communicated to us then unity in the Church will be no problem. Willing obedience to the Father. If we have the mind of Jesus then obedience to the Father will be our goal. The result of this will be unity. According to the Father's plan, Jesus left Heaven and came down to this earth. In the scriptures Jesus repeatedly says, "I came to do my Father's will." It says in Hebrews 12:1-3, Jesus willingly obeyed God in all things, eventually dying on the dreaded cross for our salvation. Jesus' example of obedience to God the Father stands for an attitude that is to be ours. We need to daily surrender ourselves to doing God's will, obeying not out of fear of judgment but because we love God. When obeying God as all things become priority, the unity in the Church will flourish.

CHAPTER SEVEN: UNITY PART ONE

4. Servanthood: When we decide to be servants of each other, according to Philippians 2:7, it speaks of Jesus taking the form of a servant. While on earth, Jesus exemplified Servanthood. Jesus said, "I came to serve not to be served." In Matthew 20:26, Jesus says whoever wishes to be great among you, must be your servant. Whoever wishes to be first among you must be your slave. Just as the Son of Man came not to be served but to serve and give His life a ransom for many.When we decide to serve one another out of love, then we will be like Christ and unity will come

5. Sacrifice and selflessness: Jesus died on the cross as a sacrifice for sins. He gave Himself for us that we might have life. In fact, Jesus died in the lowest of love ways; death on a cross. He did this for all who put their trust in Him. Jesus' sacrifice and sacrificial nature is to be imitated by us. As Jesus laid down His life for us, we must be ready to lay down our lives for one another. This will build unity and love in the Church for one another.

6. Humility: In becoming man, Jesus humbled Himself by serving others. In His death Jesus

humbled Himself by the means of the cross. When we take upon ourselves the humble attitude of Christ, then unity will thrive.
7. Waited for the Father to exalt Him: Jesus in no way sought to exalt himself. He waited and let God do that. In 1 Samuel 2:30, God says those who honor me, I will honor.

Conclusion

If we seek to exalt ourselves, it is to our shame and the lost is the unity of the Church. We must wait for God to lift us up. Greatness and honor in the Kingdom come (Removed "s" from "come") through faithful service. When we have the attitude to bring glory to God and not to ourselves, the unity will flourish in the Church.

Your **REFLECTIONS**

SIN IN THE CAMP

CHAPTER **EIGHT**
Unity: Part Two

I have a few words to add to the subject of unity. While I believe the message given by Phillip is adequate for the subject, I believe the Lord has a few more words to add to it. So here it goes.

> Unity is so very important to the body of Christ. Without it, the Church falls apart.

It is necessary to come to a place that we recognize the fact that everyone has something to contribute

SIN IN THE CAMP

to the body. We cannot leave out any part of the body because we do not think they are important.

"For as the body is one and has many members, and all the members of that one body, being many, are one body: so also is Christ. For by one Spirit are all baptized into one body, whether we be Jews or Gentiles, whether we be bond or free; and have been all made to drink into one Spirit. For the body is not one member, but many. If the foot shall say, because I am not the hand, I am not of the body; is it therefore not of the body? And if the ear shall say, because I am not the eye, I am not of the body; is it therefore not of the body? If the whole body were an eye, where were the hearing? If the whole were hearing, where were the smelling? But now hath God set the members every one of them in the body, as it has pleased him. If they were all one member, where were the body? Now are they many members, yet have one body. The eye cannot say unto the hand, I have no need of you: nor again the head to the feet, I have no need of you. Nay, much more those members of the body, which seem to be more feeble, are necessary. Those members of the body, which we think to be less honorable, upon these we bestow more honor; and our uncomely parts have more abundant comeliness. For our comely parts have no need: but God has tempered

CHAPTER EIGHT: UNITY PART TWO

the body together; having given more abundant honor to that part which lacked: that there be no schism in the body; but that the members should have the same care one for another. Whether one member suffer, all the members suffer with it; or one member be honored, all the members rejoice with it. Now you are the body of Christ, and members in particular."

1 Corinthians 12:12-27

It takes the entire body to run a well-functioning Church. While the preacher stands on the platform preaching the Word, there are those behind the stage who do the clean-up and all the little tasks that make a Church run smoothly. When the religious leaders try to control the Church, they find out the back up team leaves. Which leaves them to run everything and keep the Church clean. They find they lose valuable members as if the hand says to the foot, I do not need you.

Can you imagine a physical body trying to dictate how the body functions? It would be mass confusion. It would be like the heart coming out of the body to function as the hand and trying to grasp objects. Obviously, the heart cannot function as the hand. While there are people who have lost limbs due to birth defects, accidents, or surgery, which compensate for the lost limbs, the normal person has all his limbs which function in a normal way. You normally do not see people trying to grasp objects with their feet while their hands are used for walking. Each part does what is necessary for the part.

"There is neither Jew nor Greek, there is neither bond nor free, there is neither male nor female: for you are all on in Christ Jesus." Galatians 3:28

"Where there is neither Greek nor Jew, circumcision nor uncircumcision, Barbarian, Scythian, bond or free: but Christ is all, in all." Colossian 3:11

In these verses, Paul makes it clear that there are to be no differences between anyone in the body. We cannot exclude anyone regardless of who or what they are. When we start making distinctions, we are saying the Lord Jesus is divided. When certain groups are only to teach a certain group or perform certain functions, we are limiting the Holy Spirit.

"He gave some, apostles; and some prophets; and some evangelists; and some pastors and teachers;

CHAPTER EIGHT: UNITY PART TWO

for the perfecting of the saints, for the work of the ministry, for edifying of the body of Christ: till we all come in the unity of the faith, and the knowledge of the Son of God, to a perfect man, to the measure of the stature of the fullness of Christ: that we henceforth be no more children, tossed to and fro, and carried about with every wind of doctrine, by the sleight of men, and cunning craftiness, whereby they lie in wait to deceive; but speaking the truth in love, may grow up into him in all things, which is the head even Christ: From whom the whole body fitly joined together and compacted by that which every joint supplies, according to the effectual working in the measure of every part, makes increase of the body to the edifying of itself in love." Ephesians 4:11-16

Understand the body of Christ needs all the fivefold ministry gifts. We cannot leave out any one of them. It takes all of them to help the body function. Each gift is unique. Apostles become founders of ministries and are used to draw the body together. Prophets speak forth the Word of God, both future and present. Evangelists reach out to the lost who need to find the Lord. Pastors take these new sheep and teach them the truth

SIN IN THE CAMP

and care for the flock. Teachers teach the word to help them grow in the Lord. We have always had the gifts operating, but called by different names. Apostles were called missionaries. Prophets were called "eloquent speakers." Evangelists, pastors, and teachers were always recognized in their calling. It takes all the parts to bring the body to maturity. Despite abuses, we need to allow all the gifts to work. We need the parts to keep the false teachers out of the flock and keep the flock from getting hurt. Prophets are especially needed to correct things that are wrong. The gifts build up the Church so the flock can go out to fulfill their specific callings. Not every believer is called to these offices.

"So we, being many, are one body in Christ, and everyone members of another. Having then gifts differing according to the grace that is given to us, whether prophecy, let us prophesy according to the proportion of faith; or ministry, let us wit on our ministering: or he that teaches; or he that exhorts, on exhortation: he that gives, let him do it with simplicity; he that rules, with diligence; he that shows mercy, with cheerfulness." Romans 12:5-8

What we need to realize is, there are those

CHAPTER EIGHT: UNITY PART TWO

who are called to clean the Church; those who are called to prayer; those who are called to usher or deacon; and those who are up on the stage. Each job is important to the smooth running of the Church. Even those running the sound equipment are called to do that. It is important to realize, while all the ministries, except preaching are background ministries, without them, the ministry falls apart.

Now I am going to enter a controversial topic, but this is necessary for unity in the body. I know all the scriptures that man has used to put this group down or in specific places that they feel they belong. I am speaking of the treatment of women leaders. As Galatians says, there are neither male or female in the body of Christ. We are all called into specific ministries for a specific reason. When we say a woman is not qualified because Paul said they were to be quiet or to usurp authority, we are saying the Holy Spirit does not know what he is doing.

"Let your women keep silence in the Churches; for it is not permitted to them to speak; but they are commanded to be under obedience, as also says the law. And if they will learn anything, let them ask their husbands at home: for it is a shame for

women to speak in the Church." 1 Corinthians 14:34, 35

"Let the woman learn in silence with all subjection. But I suffer not a woman to teach, nor to usurp authority over the man, but to be in silence. For Adam was first formed, then Eve. Adam was not deceived, but the woman being deceived was in the transgression. Notwithstanding she shall be saved in childbirth, if they continue in faith and charity and holiness with sobriety." 1 Timothy 2:11-15

These two scriptures are used as clubs over women leaders. Let us examine these two scriptures.

In the first one, the Church seating was similar to a Jewish synagogue. Men and women sat apart. The women either sat on one side of the Church or in the back of the Church, while the men sat either on the other side or in front. The women hearing the truth of the Gospel wanted to know what the preacher was saying. They would shout out their questions to their husbands. This caused great confusion in the Church. Paul was telling the women to wait and ask their husbands their questions at home. This brought peace to the Church.

CHAPTER EIGHT: UNITY PART TWO

In the second passage, many women, who were cult priestesses, came out of that lifestyle to become saved. They were trying to preach the Gospel with no real understanding of what they were saying. This caused confusion. Paul wanted the women to sit down and learn the truth before they got up to speak. The other problem was these women were so used to being in charge of their temples, they tried to transfer that authority to the Church. They needed to learn submission so they could learn the truth. In the last three verses, the women were apparently leading the men back into sin, so Paul reminded the men that they needed to take authority and stop such practices. He was encouraging the women to get married and have children so they could learn to walk in holiness.

We have to balance this teaching with the teaching in the Gospel which says Mary Magdalene, a woman, was the first one to declare the resurrection of Jesus. She went to the disciples to tell them the good news. When they did not believe her, they checked out her story. They discovered she had told the truth. She and other women shared the truth so the Church could grow.

SIN IN THE CAMP

"I commend you to Phoebe our sister; which is a servant of the Church which is at Cencherea: That you receive her in the Lord, as becomes saints, and that you assist her in whatsoever business she hath need of you: for she has been a succourer of many, and of myself also." Romans 16:1, 2

Phoebe was a pastor that ministered to Paul and her congregation. Servant in the verse can mean deacon or it can mean pastor. She needed assistance to gain more knowledge and help in finding her people who were prisoners of Rome. She wanted to minister to them and return to her flock.

Men also use the text in I Timothy as an argument. They point out bishops were men who were called to lead the Church. While it is true that Paul did say men or translators said men, I believe the Lord included women in the ministry. I believe the scholars who translated the original texts went by their own biases.

"This is a true saying, if a man desire the office of a bishop, he desires a good work. A bishop then must be blameless, the husband of one woman, vigilant, sober, of good behavior, given to hospitality, apt to

CHAPTER EIGHT: UNITY PART TWO

teach; not given to wine, no striker, nor greedy of filthy lucre, but patient, not a brawler, nor covetous; one that rules his own house, having his children in subjection with all gravity; (for if a man know not how to rule his own house, how shall he take care of the church of God?) Not a novice, lest being lifted up with pride he fall into condemnation of the devil. Moreover he must have a good report of them which are without; lest he fall into reproach and the snare of the devil." 1 Timothy 3:1-7

I realize there are those who will never agree with me. But, as a part of unity, we need to be willing to agree to disagree and not harm the body by causing division over this matter. Whether we like it or not, we will have women leaders. It is time to stop relegating them to Sunday school classes of children, speaking only to women, or singing. We need to allow them to use the gifts and talents the Lord gave them to do the work they are called to.

SIN IN THE CAMP

CHAPTER EIGHT: UNITY PART TWO

Your **REFLECTIONS**

_____
_____
_____
_____
_____
_____
_____
_____
_____
_____
_____
_____
_____

SIN IN THE CAMP

CHAPTER **NINE**
Prophecy

The Lord says:

I have seen the condition of the Church. I have seen the discord, division, and confusion that is reigning in the Church. I have become very angry at the situation. I am bringing judgment to the Church.

"For the time has come that judgment must begin

at the house of God: and if it begins at us, what shall the end be of them that obey not the gospel of God." 1 Peter 4:17

My children must understand that I am tired of false teaching and twisted teaching being taught by teachers who are after money. I am sick to death of the entertainment offered in many of the "Churches" that pass for worship. They are so busy making more and more extravagant shows, they have forgotten the reason for the worship. I am to be the center of worship, not themselves.

"Nevertheless I have somewhat against you, because you have left your first love. Remember, therefore from where you are fallen, and repent, and do the first works; or else I will come unto you quickly, and will remove your candlestick out of his place, except you repent." Revelation 2:4, 5

My children have left their first love. They have forgotten I am to be the center of their lives. I desire a relationship with my children, but they have relegated me to a position of a far off God who does not care, who is a bellhop or servant. They forget that I am almighty God who came down as a human to relate to my people. As I have said in

CHAPTER NINE: PROPHECY

Isaiah, my thoughts are above the thoughts of my children and my ways are above the ways of my children.

> *"I know your works, that you are neither cold nor hot: I would you were cold or hot. So then because you are lukewarm, and neither cold or hot, I will spue you out of my mouth. Because you say, I am rich, and increased with goods, and have need of nothing; and know that you are wretched, and miserable, and poor, an blind, and naked. I counsel you to buy of me gold tried in the fire, that you may be rich; and white raiment, that you may be clothed, and that the shame of your nakedness do not appear; and anoint your eyes with eye salve, that you may see. As many as I love, I rebuke and chasten: be zealous therefore and repent."*
> *Revelation 3:15-19*

I have seen the spiritual nakedness and blindness of my children. I want to help them, but they won't let me. I am pleading with them to come back to me. I need all my children to either be hot or cold. If they are not, I will spit them out of mouth. I desire my children to be on fire for me as they are healed and clothed.

SIN IN THE CAMP

"And you have forgotten the exhortation which speaks to you as unto children, my son, do not despise the chastening of the Lord, nor faint when you are rebuked of Him: for whom the Lord loves, He chastens and scourges every son whomHe receives. If you endure chastening, God deals with you as with sons, for what son is he whom the Father chastens not? But if you be without chastisement, whereof all are partakers, then you are bastards, and not sons. Furthermore we have had fathers of our flesh which corrected us, and we give them reverence: shall we not much rather be in subjections unto the Father of spirit, and live? For they verily for a few days chastened us after their own pleasure, but He for our profit, that we might be partakers of His holiness. Now no chastening for the present seems to be joyous, but grievous: nevertheless afterward it yields the peaceable fruit of righteousness unto them which are exercised thereby," Hebrews 12:5-11

I chasten you my children because I desire to bring out the impurities in your lives. I see problems that need to be dealt with. As I deal with them, you will grow in my purity and holiness. Understand that chastisement proves you are My children. I cannot chastise those in the world because they are not mine. Just as in the natural, if an adult tries to discipline another person's child, it is called child abuse. Even so, if I discipline a child of the other kingdom, I am abusing his children.

I desire a pure and holy body. I will get that in a way that builds up the body, and not tear it down. I allow the enemy to bring tests and trials to see how you will deal with them. I want to bring you into perfection. Allow Me to do as I desire in your life.

EPILOGUE

I hope this book will help my readers realize how much the Lord desires to see a new movement towards purity. As we do what he wants, we will see a new growth in the real Church because people will flock to hear the unadulterated truth of the Word. There will be no watered-down doctrine, but the pure Word of God.

Now, I want to address my unbelieving readers. After reading this book, if you want to come to know the Lord I serve, I invite you to pray.

> Father, I repent of my sins and ask forgiveness. I accept Jesus into my heart as my personal Savior and Lord. I desire to live for you with the help of the Holy Spirit. I ask him to come and take over my life and teach and guide me into all truth. In Jesus' Name, I pray. Amen

If you prayed this prayer or something similar, I want to welcome you into the family.

Final **REFLECTIONS**

_____

_____

_____

_____

_____

_____

_____

_____

_____

_____

SIN IN THE CAMP

www.ingramcontent.com/pod-product-compliance
Lightning Source LLC
Chambersburg PA
CBHW052109110526
44592CB00013B/1541